Mind of a Nomad

Kathleen Swann

First published by Quantum Dot Press

Copyright © Kathleen Swann 2025

The right of Kathleen Swann to be identified as the author of this work has been asserted by them in accordance with the Copyright, Designs and Patents Act 1988

All characters and events in this publication, other than those clearly in the public domain are fictitious and any resemblance to real persons, living or dead is purely coincidental.

All rights reserved

No part of this publication may be reproduced, circulated, stored in a system from which it can be retrieved or transmitted in any form without the prior permission in writing of the publisher.

Book cover by Light Speed Dreams
www.lightspeeddreams.net

Mind of a Nomad

Who is the Nomad?

    The poet

    The reader

    The travels upon which the poet takes the reader

There is music in these poems as evinced by lines in the title poem 'Mind of a Nomad, which have an incantatory quality.

Geraldine Green
Poet & Tutor

For David

Some of the poems included in this book have previously been published in the following anthologies:

Creative Juices

A Chorus of Seven

New Contexts

The Raspberry & the Rowan

Seeing Things

The Other Side of the Looking Glass

This Here This Now

The poem, Down Our Street, won first prize in the Ripon Poetry Festival 2024, and gave its name to the anthology of that year.

Contents

FRAGMENTS OF HISTORY

Crossing the border	1
Mind of a Nomad	2
Saturday night, Sunday morning	4
Clandestine Marriage Book, 1745	5
After Marston Moor	6
Lily from Oswaldtwistle	7
On the Scales for Grandad	8
Organic Love	9
Minding the Gap	10
MMXX	11
The Way of Water	12
Weavers lament	14
Slim Pickings	16
Quick-step	18
Coming Home	19
The Corner Shop	20
Homecoming	22
The Ringside Seat	24
Woodsmen	26
Down our street....	28
A Cotton Office in New Orleans	30
Exiled	31
The Quarryman	32
Made to Measure in Millom	34

POSTCARDS — 37

- Burns Beck — 39
- Love affair — 40
- Stellar Moon. — 42
- Jenny Twigg and her daughter Tibb... — 44
- I am ... — 45
- The Gather — 46
- From the Watershed — 48
- Murmuration — 49
- November Snow — 50
- Eycott Lava — 51
- Green Lane to Barkin House — 52
- Tulip Fever — 54
- Modelling for Spencer Tunick — 55
- Tread Gently — 56
- Tin Soldier — 58
- Sea Chill — 59
- Worth the Effort — 60

TRANSFORMED — 63

- Corvus Girl — 65
- Systematic Disappearance — 66
- Voyager — 68
- Did the Camera Lie — 69
- Life on the Edge — 70
- Awakening — 72

Needles In Needles Out – *after Christine Cochrane*	73
Buttoned Up	74
Migration	75
Breathing Space	76
Daybreak	78
Arrival	80
Invisibility	81

JUST FOR FUN — 83

ABC of Ripon	85
The Fake Smile	86
Anything but Tripe	87
Stanza Sestina	88
Dreamboat	90
Apple Tree	91
Cash in Hand	92
Clever Devil	93
RIP Bruce	93
Acknowledgements	95
Also by Kathleen Swann	96
About Kathleen Swann	97

Fragments of History

Crossing the border

I watch her fingers pull the needle
draw thread through open weave
silk strands slip through crotchety hands
as she counts spaces   left and right
fills gaps with fragments of her life.

Age-worn eyes scan the fabric
for missed memories
do you remember, she asks, those
heat-hazed days of curlews' cries
when we walked on scrubby moorland
gazed at the far horizon,

now no light can brighten eyes
that barely see   a lifetime in a frame
a border cross-stitched   wrapped
in tissue   waiting.

Mind of a Nomad

I once knew a girl
who sold her life
for an adventure
cast aside dainty sandals
bought sturdy trainers
to tread the boards
of imagination
believed crossing
the ocean would give her
a better view

I once knew a girl
who told herself
stories of dreams
unfulfilled
left her home
in boots of fancy
to wander a world
of wild bushland
climb rugged caldera
to see far beyond

I once knew a girl
who carried her
life on her back
over mountains
down valleys
to beaches of lava
flagged down a ferryman
to row her across
the blue swaying water
to touch the horizon

I once knew a girl
who traded her comfort
to fly on a zip wire
over islands and inlets
sit at the feet of giants
run riot on a prayer wheel
breathe incense
learn karma
drink Saki

I knew this girl
she was someone

Saturday night, Sunday morning

the riverside ablaze with electric stars
from a psychedelic blur on waltzer cars
juke-box tunes spin to the speed
of my head   we fly through the night
again and again

borrowed skirts   back-combed hair
we dress to impress
for the forbidden taste of delicious risk
gone tomorrow   here today
a fairground life

another shilling   another dream ride
he spins the car   mouths the words
to Love me Do   dark hair curled
over up-turned collar   takes a comb
from the pocket of his drainpipe jeans

on the last bus   we re-live edges of danger
smouldering eyes   gravely voice
from Capstan full strength
next morning   early   the ground shakes
from the rumble of wagons
I slowly rise   tousle headed
the brown-eyed boy has moved on

Clandestine Marriage Book, 1745

The Fleet Prison
will open at ten o'clock prompt

they are barely out of childhood
as they wait nervously   hold hands
she with a single wild poppy
pinned to her plain dress
he has the required coin
imprinting its shape on his palm

the greedy-eyed priest
looks them up and down
holds out his prayer book
to receive the silver host

a sacrament in Latin
a ring   a blessing   a hurried kiss
the couple leave their names forever

Catherine Carver, age 12 Robert Baston, age 17

After Marston Moor

In the tumble of wild flowers
grown long and tangled
like an old woman's hair
a newborn moon spills light
across cracked slates
hare's breath stirs tall grasses
as the lych-gate slips its sneck
swings to and fro
in time to the march of boots
still ringing deep in the ground

clash of steel or toll of distant bell
shifting shadows slip between
gravestones glance weatherworn words
whisper long forgotten names
with a sigh that chills my bones
the uneven rhythm of feet
pass through fractured time
leave no footprint
only musket holes in sandstone

Lily from Oswaldtwistle

Passed like a parcel
brown paper   old string
a pale stem -   sprung from where
Eve's tears fell

like the seasons you move on
from town to town weighed down
by a carpet-bag of pills
pack of cards   a tatting hook

brother and sisters
jostle your arrival
as you slip into their households
but always on the edge

a folded life in a prison of guilt
trapped by the seizures
misunderstood back then
you take refuge in card games
play solitaire

On the Scales for Grandad

The costs were weighed
for the bus or train fare
and perhaps a new black hat

the people were weighed
all four of us or two
or just the one

the loss of time
from school or work
was measured and weighed

the distance was weighed
as to whether an overnight stay
would be needed

the decision was made
and my father went alone

if the depth of love had been weighed
I would have been chief mourner.

Organic Love

The house is full of the smell of yeast
a heady promise of fresh herbed bread
in these lockdown days
of hard to come-by treats.
It takes me back almost fifty years
to when bakers went on strike
queues formed for flour and yeast
when   like young birds   you were
forever hungry

In later years we made beer
homemade wine
and once again the smell of yeast
filled the recesses of our home
binding us to the garden fruit bushes
that we nurtured like children.
Now you are grown I talk to you
of sourdough and soda bread
there is comfort in swapping recipes
pooling resources
sharing home-made garlic bread and wine

Minding the Gap

You blow into the house
like the four winds
bickering, nit-picking,
arguing about dog food,
walking shoes, recycling
looking to me to take sides
affirm that one of you
is the favourite child

years between you
gives status in your minds
miles apart allows you to forget
the clan you used to be
all four of you think you know
where each of you went wrong
strangely, your sisters don't agree

but a broken washing machine
cranky car or a wrecked marriage
brings you together
you arrive with food and a bottle
bring music, tools, empathy
I know now
the distance between you
is a thread of gossamer

MMXX   *After Philip Larkin*

Those regimented lines of beds in makeshift hospitals
where music once rang out, choirs sang to audiences
seated side by side unmasked easy pleasure taken in a breath.

Long uneven lines of nurses in white suits and black humour
their names in marker pen across their chest, exhausted
by determination to understand this restless virus.

Life and death tracked on a graph, wrung out, hung to dry
in sun and wind as every year - normality in slow motion
we wait suspended in a time-warp but how long for what.

Lines of graves dug in a hurry, men with homemade masks
burrowing in the lifeless dust for those dying with no names
to be laid to rest haphazardly without a single mourner.

The Way of Water

They said.....

- there cannot be another storm like this
- the ground has no capacity for more
- the bridge is far too strong to yield
........they said.   2016

That winter constant heavy rain
eroded every crumbling fissure
assassinated walls and fences
became weightlifter for trees
forced branches into dams
as a working beaver might.

Becks to rivers filled beyond limit
fields engulfed by swirling torrents
risen above boundaries as brown-brew
sought out space to spew
its languid form with relish
claiming every place its own.

Spurting onward   heedless of time
as if late for the blocking of roads
expulsion of stones too careless
to hold on to riverbeds
drowning cars abandoned
in the scramble for safety.

Thoughtless for homes and factories
dirty liquor laps its way up walls
through kitchens   over carpets
pushes at the edges of lives
the water will be gone in days
but filth and fear linger

Weavers lament

Not a dream job this life in the mill
it's Hobson's choice for a motherless girl
      as the school gate shuts

child to adult - just a few steps
along the road in hand me downs
      piece of bread in a muslin wrap

ill-prepared for the wave of workers
surging through the factory gate
      sighs drowned in the sound of waking looms

as shuttles clack   bobbins scrape
back and forth as they weave
      jewelled threads to flowers and birds

clogs on cobbles let in the rain,
no pay if you're sick so you just carry on
      twisting fibres for loppers to slice

twelve hours a day six days a week
to pay the rent   meagre meals
        maybe a beer on Saturday night

as they mouth their words across the factory floor
women's lungs fill with shoddy air
        the foreman inhales a Havana cigar

Slim Pickings

You jam your heels
into the riser
paper thin soles
pressed
to the concrete step

knees bent
thighs tensed
fingers threaded into grooves
on the grey handle

   bump bump

the pram set off on its
precarious journey

   bump bump

at last the wheels roll onto the landing
manoeuvre into the room
joyless and cold

your brown-eyed sister
watches and waits
for bread or broth
a meagre offering

you are ten years old
none of this is your fault

Quick-step

Grey light glides over roofs
as a rising choir of birdsong
runs down the street between
the houses before sunrise

Your ringed fingers dance the dust
across age-seasoned oak,
catch it in a yellow duster
while the rest of the house sleeps.

The honeyed smell of beeswax
floats through early morning
consuming the stale night air.
Wistful songs from old films

echo round the rooms -
words drift out
on a shaft of first sunlight
as you listen to the rhythmic beat.

I hear your feet on the kitchen floor
slow-slow-quick-quick-slow.

Coming Home

Dad was like a caged bird
when he was stuck inside
always scanning the horizon

He hadn't been to our new house
everyone on their best behaviour
this was unfamiliar territory

the two of us walked
down the lane to the riverside
a place of common ground

I named the trees coming into leaf
showed him how the river
had changed its course
he was pleased that I remembered

sand martins swooped overhead
migrants returned to nest in the bank
I opened the field gate
to let my father through

The Corner Shop

Everybody knew Jimmy's,
advert for Typhoo Tea
painted in red on the window
the door hinges were stiff
but the bell still jangled to and fro
when you put your shoulder to it
a squirt of oil would have been the answer
but Jimmy didn't bother.

The smell was always the same,
fusty bread and ground coffee
on shelves full to bursting
with the same packets, tins
and boxes week in, week out
the mahogany counter cluttered
unwrapped sweets in open trays
where little fingers could just reach
mothers had no choice but to pay.

Jimmy kept a step-stool
to reach the top shelves;
if you put your order in
by Tuesday noon
he would have it boxed,
ready for delivery
on Thursday evening,
taking the time to talk
to people living on their own.

Jimmy would halve a block of butter
or sell you just one egg,
but everybody knew
he didn't give credit.

Homecoming

After his suit and briefcase
were put away for the day
he would stand
looking to the skies
Gauloise firmly clamped
between his lips
stopwatch in hand
direction and strength
of the wind
measured again.

I hadn't realised
how fickle air could be
how critical its behaviour
in the progress
of the 'favourite'
he taught me
what to look for in a champion.

When he caught sight
of a speck in the distance
he would start to whistle
high and slow
to guide his tired bird home
to be clocked
weighed   fed rich corn
him in his
dark grey overall
welcomed
a pale grey pigeon.

The Ringside Seat

was a pine pew reclaimed
from St Margaret's church
her refuge from an old
stone cottage on winter nights
hands gnarled by
continually furrowing card
her round body claimed its space

She'd talk all evening
of winters past
snow to tops of walls
farmers quartering the fell
to look for lambs
children sliding
down the icy school yard.

She told of a trip to Morecambe
once when she was young
eyes dreamy with thoughts
of candy floss and rock.
We'd heard the tales before
but this was Marilyn
old, lonely and aware of death.

After her third bottle of Stout
warmed through by a log fire
she'd heave herself from the chair
weave round the pub tables
bow to all in the room
and leave   singing.......   "What's it all about, Alfie".

Woodsmen

On the banks of the river
    where love had once waited for dark
        the aged trees fall to men
            booted and helmeted
                for heavy work

I watch plantations
    from before our time yield
        their wind-shaped crop
            to the throaty roar of a
                chain-saw

then lifted to jaw-toothed lorries
    to leave gaps
        in the forest face
            where plants lie
                in sun starved sleep

screaming steel
    in the woodyard
        fills the air
           with milky sawdust
                scent of earth planted spice

planks stacked against
    the trackside fence
        reveal the long-carved heart
            initials faded   rent in two
                in my head the Shirelles are still singing

Down our street....

  gossip is carried in shopping bags
   front doors are open and cottage walls
    listen to the chatter of the river
     this street is full of new houses
      snuggled down between the old
       settling-in as moss between boulders

dads go to work   pass the time of day
 with a hatless nod   dismissing
  the weary weather with a shrug
   as blackbirds scuttle under hedges
    and coal is carried on black-sacked backs
    to store for cooler days

wicket stumps chalked on a telegraph pole
 signal the start of summer holidays
  boys bat and girls field in and out
   of gardens   skulk behind the church
    when a death from meningitis
     leaves a hush of sadness

we are all newcomers   not yet
 steeped in the tar of this street
  unlike the farmers' sons or quarry boys
   who have worked this land
    over generations   day by day
     made this village their own

streetlights cast long shadows
 over homecoming revellers
   lingering lovers reluctantly
    unravel   to drift away
     until the seam between night and day
     frays to the rattle of milk bottles

A Cotton Office in New Orleans
By Edgar Degas

Always men, a fine mixture to be sure
going about their business
in a knowledgeable way
exercising their right to be choosy
proffering indifference
to competitors who feign relaxed interest.

Beaver hats and black wool suits, a contrast
to the accumulation of bright cotton bolls
gathered by black hands in raw sun
the teller counts his master's profit
thinks of his wage racking-up
in the kimbell's from distant sales.

A burnt sienna floor is the foil
for mahogany chairs and walls
of jersey cream or terre-verte
this painter captured his uncle's
workplace with a bustle of business
or an arrogance of waiting your turn.

Exiled

Foxgloves thrive untended
dolly mixtures in a dark corner
of a riotous garden

she takes the fell path   scissors in hand
chooses blooms the colour of sunrise
stems of the right length

for this house with wild ceilings
hand-turned spindles   criss-cross windows
which beckon views of never-ending fells

the wildness is breathtaking
a place of abundance not austerity
beauty beyond her imagination

so why does she feel abandoned
adrift   unbalanced in the quiet space
intended to set her free

can soot black walls
rough cobbled streets   mill chimneys
be her only beacon of security

The Quarryman

She loved the bones of him
her man of slate
fingers once slim and tender
now swollen from
winters of Langdale frost
forearms freckled with shale dust

she packed his bait
he riddled the fire into life
leaving at six sharp
for his lift to the mine
with men whose bodies bent
from lives of riving rock

his days spent splitting
grey green slabs of Silurian stone
weekends passed gardening or fishing
occasionally bringing back supper
she listened for the singing
of his segs along the lane

her dependable staff of life
gave her laughter and tears
made her a mother   them a family
until the day his breath ran out
their cottage felt his absence
like a gap in the earth

Made to Measure in Millom

The white line could have been
a ten-foot wall
for all the words
that crossed that street
the tailor worked
in the big white house-
laid out suiting
on a smooth oak bench
took the measure
of the men about town
in chalk and paper
shaped and cut.

Opposite the draper
bobbed up and down
answered the call
of a tinkling bell
sold cotton handkerchiefs
pairs of socks
jacket for the town-hall clerk
quality learned at his father's hands
as a youth just starting out
jealousy zipped into fabric seams
spoiled friendship
once bound in cloth.

Their children have no time
to waste on fights
when days soak up cold
from the estuary
Christmas presents
were made to share
to show from windows
on the top floor
across the space
above the white line

just a slick of paint
on a tarmac street.

From a visit to Norman Nicholson's house in Millom.

POSTCARDS

Burns Beck

    I listen to the crack of wood ticking
a clock winding on the days of spring
as my feet scrape in slow motion
over chicken-wired railway sleepers

my boots yomp in a suck of peat as we trespass
over grass and moss in a slinking fox's wake
a shimmer of myrtle feeds a myriad of bees
wasps or drifting hover flies

ethereal silver birch huddling in tranquility
are engulfed by a zephyr breeze
carrying the distant cry of a lamb
as it binds a soul in torment

water boatmen cast shadows
where cadis fly lie in wait for their time
as we take time to mend ourselves
in this rich patchwork of life

Love affair

longing pulls me back
to the sound of water
impetuously rushing over
twisted folds of rock
      draped sinuously
on the shoulder
of this roughhewn hill
a body of sediment forced upwards
in violent torment
five hundred million years ago

in my desire to clamber
over these lichen covered rocks
I have to press my fingers into the
      creases of your skin
bind my hands to your surface
as the bones of the mountains
shift their familiar shape in mist
my boot finds grip in a rib of slate
and I climb higher

anticipation of the elements
hefts me to the danger
like an old flame
      tempting me
to abandon all caution
in the exhilaration of reaching
      the summit
thrust into an ever-changing view
seen only by me
         this way
            today

Stellar Moon.

I sympathise with you   moon
  entering the stage with
    a shy smile
        not wishing to
      overwhelm the sky with your light

bolder each day   you conceal less
  on your orbital journey
    make your way through
        Perseids
          Leonids
    dodge black holes

share the sky with star shapes
    wolf
        bear
           goat
              and ram
    their earthly shadows hunted
        in silhouetted forests and fields

I take my share of your lustre
      to walk across the moor
           get your attention
                by dipping my feet
                    in the pond

      make you shiver

Jenny Twigg and her daughter Tibb...

.... live on the moor
beckon the wind
to curb the long grass
shake out brittle bracken
dry out the bogs
washed in spring rain
they preen
as the earth uncurls

.... watch the full moon
cast shadows of deer
as they weave narrow trods
in pale silky silence
she lights hollows for curlews
grassy tufts for skylark
boggy dips for frogs
in the rough freckled cloak

.... stand in all weathers
in gritstone hats
a guidepost for walkers
through mist and mizzle
a shelter for gamebirds
from the shooters
with boots and a 12 bore
who tramp over Nidderdale hills

I am ...

Norse   I spread
 my shawl of viridescence
  over sheep before shearing
   for shelter on heat-heavy days

 the medicine of a mountain
 from milk-tinged blossom
  fanned by buzzard-feathers
   down the cleft of folded rocks

a rope-clad climber that clings
 to the ledge
  of a wind torn scar
   driving fibrous roots into fissures

a fire in berries of blood
 when winter stencils
  bone-white on verglas
   after curlew and kestrel have left

  I am Caorunn
            the Rowan Tree

The Gather

backs to limestone they stand
gaberdines smudged with lambing
trace of hay   feed clinging
to tight woven fabric   buttons
rarely fastened as their minds
wander round the state of their ewes

flat caps with brims down
shelter their pipes which stutter
in Lakeland mizzle
matches doused before reaching
sweet briar-wood bowls
nicotine teeth on show at every shout

their eyes lock onto Herdwick   Swaledale
to sort their smit on each rough back
fettlin' their own with a dog and a stick
use words when they're needed
decisions in silence   sheep huddle
reluctant to part from the flock

there's talk of the wool price
new dogs and their training
hefting of lambs   winter to come
no rest in this business
there'll be no changes
their fathers   grandfathers
have hefted them too

From the Watershed

What do you taste in the granite and slate
  as you sip the flow of Gladgrove Gill
    slacken your banks in the reservoir
      to roam a lone valley of eagle   raven

    you slough the scrape of crisp marsh grass
   scorn wooded banks with dipping willow
I wake to your spit and rumble under Scroggs bridge
as you gather Hall Beck to heave and swell

into milk white waters to tumble the fall
   doff your foam by the old box mill
     breathe the woodyard   pine and paint
       greedy for growth you drink in the Gowan

     the Sprint and Mint   host to
    sticklebacks   crayfish then turn to the west
   to leave rowdy towns   drowsy villages
as you hunger for the salty taste of the sea

Murmuration

    Liquid stars weave a bone pale sky
   dancers in evening light
  swaying   shifting
balletic ripples
drift in unison
 to a whirr of wings
   whose movement is barely
    visible to the audience
    a seventh sense calls the moment when
   you gather from all four corners
  darken the shimmering sky
 how do you know which
way to go   where to turn
 when to leave for your
   homebound journey

November Snow

Even before
I open the curtains
I know

an unexpected light
belies the grey
of a winter sky at dawn

petticoat tails cling to telegraph wires
bowed by a rime of snow
scumbling through stifled air

I cross the garden like a thief
feel guilty as I break the surface
thin as spun sugar

children stir in their beds
today holds possibilities
sledging   snowball fights

winter delights
to be held precious
in an uncertain world

Eycott Lava

this stone sucks the seep of rain
  from endless skies of melting cloud
    on this restful moor of grass and bees
      in the company of butterflies
        song of curlew and raven

guardian of history beyond our knowing
  risen in caverns of molten earth
    hurled by magma into icy air
      settled in this volcanic cradle
        of sharp-edged mountains

secrets of Saxons   Romans   Vikings
  lie sleeping in your layers
    footprints melded in sandstone sills
      walk the silent ways
        to remind us one day
          we too will leave

Green Lane to Barkin House

where
I breathe warm fermenting air
rich with fruit, heavy with harvest

where
a slate sky startled by rose-hip lanterns
casts long shadows against the round-backed hill

where
grey geese rise from the reservoir   fill the valley
with raucous cries as they draw summer days away

where
a lone vetch hangs on close weave of brackens'
brown attire   amethyst on a faded frock

where
a bovine pair stand to watch trespassers
as the cry of lapwings warn of changing winds

where
willow-herb lean on the gate like old men
to watch sheep chew cud

where
pincushions of lime moss perch on through-stones
dripping nectar for field mice

where
in the distance wind turbines wave directing
traffic away from this hidden valley

     and where
I feel the descent of winter   the pull of hibernation
the need to retreat to a warm fire

Tulip Fever

frouzy   drowsy   ballgown blousy
puckered lips aflame and easy
spreadeagled stems   louche and languid
lie there defiant
        don't dare touch me

pearl-eyed petals   wan and waxy
faded sheen with fraying hems
you snare my glance as if to halt me
in my tracks
        we're not done yet

don't think we're ready for the compost
this room enslaves our gaudy light
we'll fight 'til every bowl is yawning
every stamen
        shredded dust

Modelling for Spencer Tunick

You are sun-grazed cobbles
   as you lie close
in rows of four and five
   pale hairs on your folded arms
filling the space between
   with backbones in line
shoulders   buttocks
   and hips that sway slightly
if your eyes glance sideways
   you feel alive at
five in the morning
    bodies as still as the dawn chill
when the camera shutter clicks and whirrs
   on a street of human spines
flowing to the Tyne.

Tread Gently

Runnels of earth
    slip from tramlines
   through the gaps
     in hawthorn
sculpted caverns of brambles
  guard skeletons of beech.

Beneath my feet
  leaf-mould
 shivers in decay
my breath gutters
    dusty air
  on this long-abandoned path.

Half-buried slabs of wall
    nurse star-gazey garlic
  steeped in sphagnum moss
bones of an old building
   dissolve in ivy
 sigh with
   unsung lives.

Time
    is colouring the wood
        green   white
  luminous blue
    silence and absence
are the only way markers.

Tin Soldier

You are not watching the traffic
alien vehicles   not from your time
you hold the hand of a pretty girl

her eyes on you in your uniform
your mind on this last day -
where will you fill your tin cup tomorrow

as you make your way
to the mud sodden trenches of war
her last touch of tenderness

breath of sweetness will come
to you in dreams on nights of fear
in days of fighting

for now you stand as one
captured in a cameo of stillness
traffic rushes by not watching you

Sea Chill

Thunderous tumbling surf
runs in rills among ridges of sand
reflects bruise-black clouds
which hover menacingly
above my head

a hissing wind hugs the ground
tears sand from the shore
to release pebbles like escaped souls
caught in a rogue band of sunlight

memory drifts back to beaches
of childhood digging for cockles
with plastic spade and bucket
on shifting ground
which claims many lives

chilled I am reminded
it's time to free my boots
from fast-gathering sand pools
as the horizon carries
another minute of daylight

Worth the Effort

      Slabs   worn smooth by the boots
     of seasoned coffin carriers
    now ring to the sound of my steady steps
   on the ancient track to burial
  for the labourers and farmers
from this remote valley

      Ice gouged bowl below holds
     a thousand thousand raindrops
    gathered into a dark reservoir
   to feed the distant village
  sound of the racing dam
echoes in the natural cirque.

      Ravens   only evident by their cry
     haunt crags crumbled to scree
    fallen to loneliness in the corrie
   my breath races in short soughs
  as contours narrow in shadow
the col beckons with sunlight.

Over the wind-combed moor
   stones give way to cotton grass
    long haired   short legged ponies
  grazing scrub and rank grasses
 welcome my arrival with
sweet steaming breath from putty lips.

TRANSFORMED

Corvus Girl

She is crow

wraithlike shape perched

on rough black rocks

calls to the sky with dry parched voice

windswept ragged coat unravels

shreds peel to cloud

swirl into feathers

form into wings

lift her to air

fly

Systematic Disappearance

The system was his undoing
its need to be fed with information
that he didn't have
a date of birth from so long ago
he had left it behind   somewhere
between the school walls
and a job on the railways

It required figures and numbers
generated on documents
which needed to be filed   so that
when the system was floundering
it could request him to open the box
at random   to top up the weight of
data that verified his existence

For years he had addresses
where electricity bills could land
on a mat which said   'welcome'
although they never were
but circumstances forced him
to move   to hedgerows or doorways
not acceptable to the system

He slipped into being a non-person
ignored with studied effort
passed by at leprotic distance
a homeless man
a temporary patient
a body for a pauper's funeral
buried with the other unclaimed dead

Voyager

Spring has been impatient for your arrival
searched sandbanks   scanned the skies
for your moleskin wings
skimming telephone wires.

You call to each other as
you arrive in days stretched beyond
a waning moon   perform aerobatics
against a blue and orange sky.

I wake early today, you are lying on the path
your soft cream underbelly unmarked
for a moment I hope you're just stunned
but I know you are lifeless.

You travelled so far to raise your young
I can't bear to see your death on my stones
I carry you to a silent place   let your body
melt into the mossy ground.

Did the Camera Lie

The photograph falls
from the pages
of a poetry book

a careless glance and I'm
surprised to see my mother
leaning forward

left shoulder raised
to allow her arm
to wrap a young woman
in a warm embrace

shoulders tense
she leans in to the returned hug
a curl of grey hair
square chin
ample cheek pressed close
in a smile of pleasure

I am confused about time and place
and look more carefully
as I remember
I went to this reading alone

Life on the Edge

We ran in and out
of the shells
of new houses,
    carefree
    in shorts and sandals
the building site
our playground
hide and seek
in hollow rooms
    echoey voices
    count slowly
laugh in the riot
of new council homes

You stare at the shells
of houses
    powerless
    in your tattered
    clothes
you sit on the step
    where a door once stood
dust filled desolation
    drowned by bombs
you count

    losses

    deaths

    destruction

sit in the dust with your doll

her eyes covered

Awakening

Towards night a woodpecker
tolls the death of an old oak
a star blinks through deepening shadows
from deep in my dreams
night is stirring
with the call of an owl
who is beckoning me
from my rest
already I have begun
the long climb to meet him

Needles In Needles Out – *after Christine Cochrane*

I hand over my reel of cotton   packet of needles
'did you get everything you wanted today', she asks
I nod - but I want to say – not really – I would like to house
the homeless man sitting outside the supermarket
or find a solution for refugees camping in Calais
I'd really like to help the woman who was beaten
by her husband and left home in the middle of the night
with nothing but her children

I long to see government ministers with families
manage for a year on universal credit
in a flat on the seventeenth floor
when the lift is out of order
I'm not in favour of paying huge bonuses
to failing company bosses and don't get
me started on Brexit, Rwanda
or NHS pay and dentistry

but none of the solutions to these problems
are available in Yorkshire Trading
so I nod again and thank the woman
leave the shop with my domestic repair kit
ready to mend just one thing today.

Buttoned Up

Ivory   bone   mother-of-pearl
buttons spill on to the table
her fingers shuffle them into colours
as a magician stirs dice
to confound the watcher

Memories rise from cotton threads
drift from a scrap of work-shirt
with the smell of brick dust   sand   cement
the feel of his ingrained hands
 a map of the day's toil

alone in her house
with walls he mended
roof he fixed
she learns to patch up cracks
share space with his treasures
from buildings and beaches

what had reason once
now has history so deep
she lives on the flotsam

Migration

They remember
the taste of the river
the smell of gravel
as familiar as instinct
that pulls them
through cold heavy seas
to feel an old acquaintance
with sunlit pools
in salt free water
buffering against autumn
the narrows of gorges
challenges of cataracts
to the place of spawning
changed from grey to red
in the reed bed of birth
homecoming.

Breathing Space

automated doors
    suck fresh air from his skin
take the cool breath
    from his lips
in a place of anxiety
    with a buzz of questions
thrown at a girl
    who looks as if she knows
follow the red line
    he's told   conscientiously
he steps heel to toe along
    a coloured ribbon of paint
down a diminishing corridor

    a clerk carries folders
tight to her breast
    he holds his fear
silent in his chest
    as the scanner moves
over his taut body
    flashing bright lights
with a rhythmic pulse

    everyone smiles as he
prepares to leave
    with no answer to
the question hanging on his lips
    phone your doctor
in a week   he doesn't
    understand why it takes so long
but he follows the line
    to the automated door
breathes the cool fresh air

Daybreak

I am a statue in my wicker chair
in the room of windows
waiting
to catch that moment when the house
slides from night into morning

while the moon drifts slowly west
the sky glows in front of me
the garden orchestra rises
from whisper to chorus

as the sun becomes
a fiery ribbon along the horizon
and the earth falls
into the warmth of a new morning

I want to slow it down
 to stop it
just for an instant to still the day
as new and fresh as every birth

how was it decided that today
became yesterday and
yet tomorrow
drifts into today

I want to be there
in that second
when ice is no longer ice
but isn't yet water

Arrival

It is a silent birth
 a slow emergence
  without fanfare,
   just a rhythmic pulse
    pushed to the light
    from deep under,
marsh grass bends
before its clarity
it's cool persistence,
'til it nudges shale stones
 catches dew from devils-bit scabious
  and raindrops
   from larch trees bowing
    bony fingers
    to damsel flies,
grey wagtails dip
on newly formed sand banks
everything is possible
there will be fish   frogs
 farms   people
  you can hear it
   approaching on the wind,
the valley sings for
the arrival
of new life

Invisibility

When alone I become invisible
sink into the quiet me
who stands and stares
at the bee sucking nectar
a goldfinch fighting for a share of seeds
I can meld in time to when I lived in the wild
listening to the sounds of leaves
chattering to the wind
I can fly to the future for the life I hope to have
Being invisible allows me
to step out of expectation

Just for Fun

ABC of Ripon

Anyone would think it impossible
But can you imagine your home
Cascading
Down a hole
Each red brick
Falling down a chasm that occurs in the
Gypsum a
House hidden
In the space you were preparing to plant parsley
Just as you went to fill the
Kettle to blanch the soil
Lo and behold a
Massive cave
Newly formed
Opened up and the front wall
Plummeted into the crack, the
Question is can it be
Rebuilt on the existing
Site, after all parts of
This city are known to be
Unstable or at the
Very least
Wobbly
X-rays may reveal more but for the minute
You are ground
Zero

The Fake Smile

starts with the teeth
white shards make their debut
as the scarlet lipsticked top lip
lifts   straightens   pushes
cotton wool cheeks towards the ears
pulls the bottom lip sideways
whisker-like strokes form
on a matt landscape
contort the lower
portion of the face
this movement stops
just above the nostrils
eyes remain untouched

I reciprocate

Anything but Tripe

I like a plate of jellied eels
or shrimps on buttered toast
black pudding is a favourite dish
and ham hock if its roast

I'd set upon a hotpot
with dumplings lightly spiced
or brisket rolled and boiled with veg
if very thinly sliced

devilled kidneys on a skewer
dripping with hot butter
kippers lightly smoked on oak
fattening I hear you mutter

a dish of liver lightly fried
with onions brown and sweet
pressed ox-tongue with pickled veg
that really is a treat

I'm not a fussy eater
I've a healthy appetite
so you can give me anything………
well anything but tripe

Stanza Sestina

The leader sent a message on email
inviting poets to meet up at a pub
bring a sheaf of papers with a poem
to share with other critics in the room
they travelled far and wide to join the throng
set in to monthly gatherings of toil.

At first the overriding thing was toil
when the message came out over the email
but then we got to know each of the throng
who made that Monday journey to the pub
to meet upstairs in that cold dining room
share our precious work, the monthly poem.

Each of us worked on our own style of poem
for which we sweated lots of tears and toil
brought copies in a folder to the room
in answer to the invite on email
we'd drive through wind and weather to the pub
to join the now familiar friendly throng.

Some have joined and others left the throng
working every month on a new poem
enjoying food and beverage in the pub
which helps to ease the tension and the toil
that one can feel when reading that email
summoned to a meeting in the room.

Some winters there was fire in the room
which warmed the hearts and bodies of the throng
responding to the message on email
relaxed voices for reading out the poem
soothed the anticipation of the toil
when sitting in that large room in the pub

For two years we have not met in the pub
our meetings have been held in our own room
one of the group has taken on the toil
and so the trust has built within the throng
that they will receive each writer's poem
arriving with a photo on email.

We hope the pub will welcome back the throng
in our familiar room to read our poem
no longer dread the toil when seeing that email.

Dreamboat

The instrument
is a silver boat
playing the blues
on arrowed bows
   songs of the salty sea
   vibrate the air
   as halyards sing
   to birds in the sky
   pebbles rattle response
you may feel
sailcloths beat out
notes of memories
plucked from the tips
of rolling waves
   keeping time
   with sailors of the deep
   echoing shanties
   on a coralline floor
fingers of musical time play
the keys of jazz
as you hear
whispers of voyagers
travel in harmony
   with a circus
   of porpoise
   sea swallow
   gannet

Apple Tree

Apples fall, I pick them up
   more then fall, I pick them up

each day they fall, I pick them up
   birds peck at some, I pick them up

winds loosen lots, I pick them up
   give some away and pick up more

I cook a lot and bag up more
   make bottles of juice from those I pick

but yet still more for baking, pies,
   crumbles, cake and more

they fall like leaves, I rake them up
   they land in flowers, I take them up

and throw them on the compost heap,
   the garden bin, the council tip

was the apple tree in Eden
   so prolific

Cash in Hand

I'll keep my money in a tin
and when I'm old if my hair
grows thin I'll buy a wig - be
a blonde and wear red
lipstick

I'll keep my money in a jar
so if I need some high heeled
shoes in azure blue or smokey grey
I'll buy them whatever they
may say

I'll put my money in a box then
if I want to rent a car in racy green
with open top and silver wheels
I'll hit the open road in style
and smile

I'll put my money in a sack
for when I'm feeling daring
buy a helmet   shiny black
to match the leather jacket
go hang-gliding

Clever Devil

RIP Bruce

The devil makes work for idle hands
with paper clips and rubber bands
origami frogs and birds
the chairman's voice is hardly heard.

He whispers in my ear, just look
that fellow there is reading a book
I concentrate with my sternest face
and wonder why I sat in this place.

I hear the voice of the councillor bold
who wants to know why we won't be told
that he is right and we are wrong
the devil is humming a silly song.

Just when I feel this is my nightmare
he says his piece and makes everyone stare.
He died too early, just left us one night
that devil, the doctor who knew what was right.

From the proverb "The devil makes work for idle hands

Acknowledgements

My thanks go to the poet friends from U3A Scriveners Group, North Yorkshire Stanza Group, the Farm Group, Ripon Writers Group and the Arvon Group for their unfailing support and encouragement in the writing and editing of many of these poems.

Thank you to Dr Geraldine Green for taking the time to read this collection, and her expertise in commenting generously on the content.

My family and friends, past and present, often provide the inspiration for a poem. Although they may not identify themselves, I am pleased to incorporate them in my work. Thank you to my husband, David, for his continual encouragement and support.

Also by Kathleen Swann

Ripples Beyond the Pool
Coverstory Books, 2019
Phyll to Her Friends
Quantum Dot Press, 2022

About Kathleen Swann

Kathleen was born in West Yorkshire but brought up in The Lake District. She wrote for the school magazine and enjoyed making up stories for local children and the children she cared for when she worked as an au pair in Brussels.

Having worked in the NHS in North Yorkshire for twenty-six years, where writing board papers and clinical reports were her daily routine, she promised herself that when she retired, she would return to writing and storytelling for her own pleasure.

Her first book of poetry, Ripples Beyond the Pool, was published in 2019. Her poems have been included in a wide range of anthologies for over ten years.

She joined the local U3A Family History group and researched her mother's family back through many generations. This led to the publication of her biography, Phyll to her Friends, in 2022.

This second book of poetry, Mind of a Nomad, roams around the people and places she has lived and visited.

Kathleen still lives in North Yorkshire, and when she is not writing, she enjoys gardening, cooking, socialising with friends, and goes to a weekly dance class.